In Spirit and Truth

In Spirit and Truth

Prayers for Worshipers

Susan L. Gleason

WIPF & STOCK · Eugene, Oregon

IN SPIRIT AND TRUTH
Prayers for Worshipers

Wipf & Stock
An Imprint of Wipf and Stock Publishers
199 W. 8th Ave., Suite 3
Eugene, OR 97401

www.wipfandstock.com

PAPERBACK ISBN: 978-1-4982-9471-3
HARDCOVER ISBN: 978-1-4982-9473-7
EBOOK ISBN: 978-1-4982-9472-0

Manufactured in the U.S.A.   09/01/16

An earlier version of "Ruler of Heaven" was previously published as "Ruler of Heaven" in *Alive Now*, March/April, 2010. "Prayer for Those in Military Service" was previously published as "A Prayer for Departing Soldiers" in *Alive Now*, March/April 2009, and "Prayer for Peacemaking" was previously published as "May Peace Prevail" in *Alive Now*, November/December, 2013.

If the only prayer you said was "thank you,"
that would be enough.

—MEISTER ECKHART

This book is dedicated, with love and gratitude,

To the memory of my parents, William J. and F. Patricia
Gleason, who taught me to pray and stood at my bedside each
night as I knelt to say my childhood prayers,

And to those whose devotion to prayer and service have been
an inspiration:

My uncle and godmother, William (Buddy) and Ann Dwyer,

And my mother-in-law, Nancy H. Sechrest.

Contents

Preface

"AND REMEMBER, SUNDAY COMES every four days." These words, spoken in jest to a seminarian about to enter the pastorate, ring true for every minister and worship team entrusted with the task of preparing meaningful worship services on a weekly basis. No sooner has the pastor bestowed this week's benediction than next week's call to worship is waiting to be written. *In Spirit and Truth* aims to assist pastors and worship planners by providing thoughtful, expressive prayers that combine traditional, reformed liturgical forms with contemporary, relevant expressions of praise and need.

In John 4:23, Jesus tells a Samaritan woman, "the true worshipers will worship the Father in spirit and truth . . ." In worship, we hope to learn and express truth as we seek unity with the God we glorify. But our human weakness interferes, for as the Apostle Paul avers, "We do not know how to pray, as we ought" (Rom 8:26). However, we are aided by the Spirit, whom Paul tells us "intercedes with sighs too deep for words" (Rom 8:26). The prayers within our worship services are, therefore, part of the ongoing Spirit-assisted conversation through which we come to know God's will and way as we call upon God to forgive our mistakes, to increase our understanding, and to direct our lives. *In Spirit and Truth* is a compilation of prayers meant to serve those who are faithfully engaged in facilitating the human end of that conversation.

Acknowledgements

I would like to thank my dear friends in the First Presbyterian Church of McMinnville, Oregon; the First Presbyterian Church of Haverhill, Massachusetts; and the Presbyterian Church (USA) in Clinton, Massachusetts, for fostering my writing and my ministry.

Special thanks go to Jennifer Dickinson, also known as "Fabulous Jenn," who kept a file of my prayers and began the collection that became this book.

To my mentors Randy Steele and Eric Markman, I appreciate the experience you shared and the opportunities you graciously afforded me to participate in worship planning and leading.

I am grateful to my cherished friend Kim Zinsser, who throughout the writing of this book was the voice of thoughtful reflection and understanding at the other end of the phone.

I would also like to recognize my Spiritual Director, Susan Troy, who has graced me with her wisdom and encouragement. Her influence may be seen throughout these pages.

The enthusiasm and support of my family is a blessing beyond measure. Thanks go to my daughters, Rachel and Emily, and also to my son and son-in-law, Colin and Yeison. You are always in my prayers along with our darling Thea, whose antics never fail to delight and often keep me going.

And, as always, I am thankful for the generous help and unfailing support of my partner in all things, my loving and beloved husband, Charlie Monroe, without whom the manuscript (and a lot of other things) might never have been finished.

1

Enter His Gates

Prayers for Preparation

Enter his gates with thanksgiving, and his courts with praise.
Give thanks to him, bless his name.

—Ps 100:4

THE BEGINNING OF WORSHIP often finds stragglers making their
way to the pews; visitors gazing at their surroundings, unsure of
what to expect; friends recounting the week's events; and parents
trying to calm already-restless children. The following Prayers for
Preparation may be printed in the bulletin as a device for helping worshipers center themselves before the introit or announce-
ments, or they may serve as the opening words of worship spoken
aloud by the leader, letting the congregation know that it is time
to put aside distractions and become focused. These first prayers
include petitions for the presence of the Holy, and they express
hope for the fulfillment of our longing to know and serve the One
who has gathered us together. Prayers for services where the Lord's
Supper will be celebrated, as well as for specific Sundays, are at the
end of the chapter.

In this time of worship, O God, refresh our desert hearts with living water. Pour out your Holy Spirit on us, and fill us with joy and peace. Then send us out into the world to spill your good news everywhere. Amen.

❧

In the silence and the singing, in the praying and the listening, in the giving and receiving, be present here. In the hand that shares your peace, in the voice that speaks your Word, in the instrument that plays your praise, be present here. So fill this place that we may not fail to see and hear you whom we seek. So fill our hearts that we may not fail to be moved to give you thanks and glory. We pray in Jesus's name. Amen.

❧

Almighty God, you sent Jesus to proclaim your reign and to teach with authority. Anoint us with your Spirit so that we too may bring good news to the poor, bind up the brokenhearted, and proclaim liberty to the captive, through Jesus Christ our Lord, who lives in unity with you and the Holy Spirit, one God, now and forever. Amen.

❧

Holy God, as we gather this day to praise and worship you, we rejoice that you are a God who does not stand at a distance, but who comes near and calls us into relationship with you. You call us into covenant and give us your Word of wisdom so that we might live lives wholly pleasing to you. Open our hearts so that we may hear your Word and claim your promises in Jesus's name. Amen.

❧

Spirit of God, inspire us, indwell us, and inform us so that your ways, your will, and your wisdom might be known to us and through us. As we gather in Christ's name, open our ears to your teaching, our eyes to your truth, and our hearts to your leading. By your presence here, unite us in faith and purpose. Amen.

❧

Jesus, you promised your people an advocate to be with us forever as a Spirit of Truth. Grant that, as we gather, we may be governed by that Spirit so that our words, thoughts, and actions might reveal the One who calls us to this place and in whose name we pray. Amen.

❧

God of Promises Kept, as we gather this day, give us the faith to believe that, by your grace, our mourning may be turned to dancing, our darkness made bright, and our hopes fulfilled in miraculous ways. Fill us with faith, with wonder, and with awe so that this sanctuary may truly become holy ground. Amen.

❧

As we gather in your holy presence, O Divine Counselor, teach us the language of love. As your Word fills our hearts, let wisdom direct our understanding so that we, in speech and action, may share your message of truth and justice. In Christ's name, we pray. Amen.

❧

This day, O Giver of Good Gifts, as we gather in this sacred place, grant that we may be willing to put down our preconceptions and our prejudices; to let go of our selfishness and senselessness; and to reach out to receive your Word and your wisdom, your light and your love. Let reflection lead to restoration; let prayer inspire preparedness; let fellowship in the Spirit beget faithful service and discipleship so that you may be glorified. In Jesus's name, we pray. Amen.

❧

God of Surprises, when we want to remain in the confines of our comfortable understanding, open us to the wideness of your mercy and the depth of your grace. Amen.

❧

God of Our Lives, we give ourselves to you in praise. Open our eyes to your glory, our ears to your Word, our hearts to your love, our minds to your mystery, and our lives to your leading so that we may be wholly thine. Amen.

❧

Jesus, even as you filled the nets of the fishermen in ways that brought wonder and awe, so fill us with amazement at your presence and your bountiful grace so that we too will follow you faithfully. Amen.

❧

Holy Spirit, dove descending,
bless me with the news that I too am God's child,
pleasing and washed clean of all that is abhorrent in God's sight.
In my time of testing,
grant faithfulness and strength;
or, if I fail, give restoration grace.
Holy Spirit, dove descending,
fill me with the hope of new beginnings in Christ Jesus,
who promises my desert soul will thirst no more. Amen.

❧

God, you see all and know all. We ask that you would help us to see and to know your ways. We come seeking wisdom and grace, forgiveness and hope. Help us to look at the world through your eyes; help us to find the dark places where your light of truth must be shown; help us to envision the kingdom as you would have it be; and grant that we may respond to the vision you give us in ways that will bring us face-to-face with Love. Amen.

❧

Lord, even as a humble servant anointed you with her precious gift of perfume, so let us kneel before you and offer what we have to give. Help us to be generous in the giving and, by your grace, let us know that we have done well in your sight. Amen.

❧

Creator God, Sustainer of all living things, we gather here aware of our need for healing and certain of your abiding grace. When Jesus offers to change our lives, help us to say yes and to rise and walk in new ways, giving thanks and glory to you. Amen.

❧

Jesus, by your grace,
let us rise above the pettiness of this world,
and follow you to a place where wisdom and peace abide.
Bring us into your healing, holy presence,
and make us one with truth and light,
to the glory of your precious name. Amen.

❧

Creator God, even as the trees in many-colored splendor reach heavenward,
so let us raise holy hands to you.
Even as the birds of the air glorify you with songs of praise,
so let us lift our voices in awe and joy.
Even as your almighty hand changes the seasons,
so change our hearts that, by your grace,
we may enter your sanctuary in the spirit of thanksgiving and righteousness.
In Christ's name, we pray. Amen.

❧

Great Physician, put your healing hand upon us and upon our world. Tend the sick at heart, restore the wounded spirit, give rest to the weary, and peace to the embattled. And, as you amend our brokenness, may worship and praise be our response to the power and love of your ministrations. Make us whole and wholly yours. In Christ's name, we pray. Amen.

❧

Lord, we come to this place calling for your truth, in need of your holy, healing presence. We come with hearts wide open, eager for the Spirit's anointing. By your grace, may we be filled with the hope and the love that are eternal. And, even as you fill us, prepare us to pour out your gifts to others. In Jesus's name, we pray. Amen.

❧

God of Grace and Peace, your presence is our source of delight. Be with us here as we gather to sing, to pray, and to be united by your boundless love. Inspire us, so that we may have the mind of the One who gathers us here. Encourage us, so that we may open our hearts to your will. Empower us, so that we may have the strength to do the work of your holy church. In Christ's name, we pray. Amen.

❧

As we gather in your holy presence, singing, "Come Lord Jesus," may our hearts be devoted places of welcome and our lives sincere witnesses to your transformational love, so that all who enter this sacred space may come to know you, Giver of Eternal Life and Sustainer of the Faithful. We pray in Christ's name. Amen.

❧

Holy God, grant that in all things we will be eager to serve not ourselves, but you. Guide us in the ways of kindness, grace, generosity, and peace. Help us to envision a world where all people are afforded dignity and hope, where justice is served, and where righteousness reigns. Then give us the courage to do our part in the realization of that glorious vision through the power of your Holy Spirit. Amen.

❧

Let me take this time, O God, to listen to the still, small voice within. Take away the distractions that interrupt my conversation with you. When I hear you say, "Your sins are forgiven," let me embrace the freedom and peace that those words afford. When I hear you say, "Come to the table," let me break bread with love in my heart for all who are at the table with me. When I hear you say, "Go forth and make disciples," let me renew my commitment to share your good news through my words and actions. Help me to listen carefully and to respond graciously. Amen.

&

Let gratitude be the root of my prayers, the source of my perspective, and the foundation of my lifestyle so that my silence, my words, my stillness, and my actions may continually praise the One from whom all blessings flow. Amen.

&

Holy God, may all who enter this sacred space find the charity, the grace, and the truth that unite us as your family of faith. Remind us that it is better to be kind than right, that it is better to be fair than first, and that it is better to have love than luxuries. Help us to reach out to all your children in ways that say we are united in Christ, in whose name we pray. Amen.

&

Shepherd God, throughout our faith journeys, lead us to places where hope is renewed, understanding deepened, inspiration awakened, and vision made clear. Walk with us, help us to recognize your holy truth, and fill us with the desire to proclaim it in word and deed so that you may be glorified. Amen.

&

Lord, when my heart is troubled, help me to remember that you are the Way, the Truth, and the Life so that I may journey not in fear, but faithfully to the place you have prepared. In your holy name, I pray. Amen.

&

May the Creator of all things be with us here as we seek to live according to the teachings of the Savior through the inspiration of the Spirit. May the triune God inform our minds, transform our hearts, and reform our lives so that we may serve God and God's children faithfully. Amen.

❧

In the choices of each day, O Lord, strengthen us so that we may follow the ways of the Spirit and choose the freedom of love and forgiveness, not the slavery of pride and materialism. Help us to hear your call in the cries of the poor and the lonely and to answer with words and deeds that witness to the saving grace of Christ, in whose name we pray. Amen.

❧

Gracious One, you hear the prayers of the world: prayers for help, prayers of hope, prayers for peace, and anguished cries for mercy, safety, and relief. Use us to answer a prayer in the name of the Creator, and of the Christ, and of the Holy Spirit. Amen.

❧

O God, in your hand, a loaf of bread becomes a feast for thousands. Help us to trust in your provision, bless us, and enable us to joyfully share what we receive so that you might be served and glorified. In your holy name, we pray. Amen.

❧

Jesus, help me always to know and to say that you are God's Promised Redeemer, the Holy One, who harbors my hopes, heals my hurts, and holds my heart. May I be a faithful follower, proclaimer of your truth, practitioner of your justice, and bearer of your good news to the glory of God and the preservation of the kingdom. In your blessed name, I pray. Amen.

❧

Creator and Ruler of the Universe, help us to see the world anew. Let us look for what unites us as your children;

let us listen with compassion to the pain and anger in each other's sighs;

let us reach across false divisions to grasp an understanding of your divine plan for us;

let us speak words of hope and walk in paths of righteousness so that peace and justice may prevail and all may know abundant life.

In your holy name, we pray. Amen.

❧

Loving God, grant me the patience to move according to your plan and not according to my vain desires. Grant me faith to know that you are with me even when I do not recognize your presence. Give me a contrite heart when I accept this world's deceptions and abandon your divine truth. Let me not seek to mold you according to my very human requirements, but rather let me be willing to have you make of me all that you intend. In Jesus's name, I pray. Amen.

❧

Holy God, we are here to speak:
a word of thanks, a plea for forgiveness, a creedal confirmation.
And we are here to listen:
for words of wisdom, for your call to act, for the promise of salvation.
And we are here to sing:
songs of praise, psalms of longing, hymns of sacred history.
And we are here to share:
the gifts you have given, the faith you inspire, the hope that is born whenever we gather in your precious name.
Lover of Our Souls, hear, speak, receive, and bless.
Be glorified! Amen.

❧

Gracious God, strengthen my faith so that the life I lead will affirm that I am freed by your promises. In responding to Christ's call and following his example, may I be prayerful, generous, truthful, merciful, and justice-seeking. Guide my steps, guard my tongue, heal my heart, and help my unbelief, in the name of Love Incarnate. Amen.

&

Write your message, O God, on the slate of my heart; teach me the language of love and help me to read, with insight and right-mindedness, your divine Word. Let me be an apt pupil, attentive and devoted, so that I may live according to your will and your way. In Jesus's name, I pray. Amen.

&

Divine Counselor, teach me the art of embracing mystery. Help me to seek truth, not merely to collect facts. Give me the faith to believe what my heart perceives, not only what my senses acknowledge. Allow me to trust this joy that rises and calls forth songs and praise. Open my heart so that Jesus may find in it a welcoming place from which to set the heavens rejoicing anew. Amen.

For When the Lord's Supper Will Be Celebrated

Giver of Life, as we gather in this place to hear and contemplate your Word and to share in the fellowship of bread and wine, grant that we may be nurtured and sustained. Fill us with enough truth to make us courageous, enough grace to keep us humble, and enough love to compel us to go and tell others of the One whose generous hand feeds us. Amen.

&

Call us into your presence, O Lord; feed us; enfold us in your loving arms; and, when we have rested there awhile, awaken in us your holy call to feed others and to lead them home. Amen.

&

Feed me with the bread of heaven, fill me with the wine of truth, bless me with abundant faith, and grant me hope and joy, O Lord. I hunger and thirst for you! Amen.

For the Day and Week After Christmas

Though the stars fade in the dawn of the new day, still the promise of the Bethlehem star burns bright in our hearts. God is with us! Let our grateful lives bear witness to our faith in the One who came and is coming. Let the light of God's love shine in and through us, bringing comfort and good news to all. In Christ's name, we pray. Amen.

For the First Sunday of the New Year

God of New Beginnings, help us to put behind us all that is not of you. Let your Spirit move among us, bringing renewed hope and restored faith that the coming year may be one in which we live lives obedient to your commandments and receptive to your Word. May we carry with us each day the wonder and delight found at the manger and the light of God's abiding love. In Jesus's name, we pray. Amen.

For Transfiguration Sunday

Creator God, we gather before you as servants awaiting the commandments of the Master, as children seeking a guiding hand, as the lost who are eager to be found. This day, lead us to that place where we may see, hear, and be transformed so as to become radiant bearers of your amazing truth and abiding love. We pray in Jesus's holy name. Amen.

For Ash Wednesday

O Jesus, give your followers hope enough to embark on this sacred journey, vision enough to see the path on which you lead us, faith enough to keep going when the way is frightening, strength enough to bear the crosses we are given, and wisdom to know that, by your grace, love and life will triumph. Amen.

For Holy Week

Lover of My Soul, I weep when I consider the trials and pain you endured for me. It is only by the transforming power of your love that I am worthy to be called a child of God and to know the comfort of my inheritance in you. Grant that I may accept that comfort with gratitude and that, in your name, I may comfort those who mourn. Amen.

❧

Jesus, I have not the strength to carry my cross alone. I need you to walk with me each step of the way, so that I will not stray from the path of righteousness. When I stumble, or worse, become a stumbling block for others, forgive me and with gentle hands restore me to your Way so that I may assuredly find the place you are, even now, preparing for me. Amen.

❧

Ruler of Heaven,
They gave you a crown of thorns and called you "King of the Jews."
They whipped you like a slave, mocked you, and waited for you to
fall in weakness.
Yet you rose in strength to sit at the right hand of God.
Threatened with bodily harm, you promised spiritual healing.
Led to a place of death, you showed the way to eternal life.
Jesus, I long to turn things around as you do.
Teach me to see your truth through the lies of this world.
Teach me to find faith in an era of doubt.
Teach me to hold on to goodness when evil is loosed.
Teach me to be like you. Amen.

For Maundy Thursday

Jesus, even as your disciples gathered for the Passover meal centuries ago to remember God's beneficence in the fulfillment of divine promises, so too are we here to remember. We ask that as we gather in your name, you will be here with us. As we break bread, share the cup, and tell of your sacrifice of love, inspire and empower us. Give us the faith and courage to respond in bold and meaningful ways to your commandment that we love one another as you have loved us, so that you may be glorified. In your holy name, we pray. Amen.

For Easter Sunday

Even as the stone was rolled away, let all that distracts me from embracing the good news of this day be shifted until I see clearly the awesome truth that death has been conquered. Then let me boldly share the gospel, crying out with angels and with all of creation, "Alleluia! Jesus lives!" Amen.

For Easter Season

Shepherd God, your love for us led you to the cross. In this season of resurrection and renewal, restore our love for you so that we might take up our crosses gladly and follow you. Renew our hope so that we may face each day believing you have prepared a place for us. Renew our faith so that we may believe you will lead us to that place, a home of eternal peace and communion with God. Teach us, your sheep, to know your voice, to trust in your goodness, and to let you find and hold us. Amen.

2

Come Let Us Worship

Calls to Worship

O come, let us worship and bow down: let us kneel
before the Lord, our Maker

—Ps 95:6

A COLLECTION OF RESPONSIVE prayers calls the worshipers to rejoice in the presence of the Eternal. These prayers celebrate the Trinity and the power of the Almighty while inviting members of the congregation to express gratitude, to offer their gifts, and to make their petitions known. Some of these prayers befit a particular day of worship (e.g., when the Lord's Supper is celebrated), others are suited to a season of the year, and still others may be used any time the family of God assembles for worship.

IN SPIRIT AND TRUTH

Leader: When fear is great and faith is small and we do not know where to turn,

Congregation: our help is in the name of the Lord, who made heaven and earth.

Leader: When spirits are low and anxieties are high and we do not know whom to trust,

Congregation: our help is in the name of the Lord, who made heaven and earth.

Leader: When temptation is strong and resolve is weak and we do not know how to choose,

Congregation: our help is in the name of the Lord, who made heaven and earth.

Leader: Wherever we go, whatever we do, whenever we are in need of guidance,

Congregation: our help is in the name of the Lord, who made heaven and earth.

Leader: Let us sing our praise and thanks to the One who is our ever-present source of help.

All: Let us worship God—Creator, Sustainer, and Friend. Amen.

❧

Leader: For the earthly ministry of Jesus, who taught with authority, in truth, and in love,

Congregation: we give you thanks, O God.

Leader: For the Holy Spirit, who inspired the apostles and has guided your people from age to age,

Congregation: we give you thanks, O God.

Leader: For the saints and martyrs who lived and died spreading the good news with courage and faith,

Congregation: we give you thanks, O God.

Leader: For the missionaries and teachers who continue to encourage others to turn to you,

Congregation: we give you thanks, O God.

Leader: As we learn to be discerning students and witnesses to Christ, the fulfillment of your holy promises,

Congregation: we give you thanks, O God.

Leader: Let us give thanks and praise to the Giver of All Good Gifts.

All: Let us worship God. Amen.

❧

Leader: The Savior says, "Take and eat."

Congregation: May we be nurtured and sustained by what we receive here.

Leader: The Redeemer says, "Drink."

Congregation: May we be refreshed and renewed by what is poured out for us this day.

Leader: The Messiah says, "Do this in remembrance of me."

Congregation: May we who gather in Christ's name proclaim again our gratitude and our hope.

All: Let us worship and adore. Amen.

❧

Leader: The God of Creation is building an eternal dwelling and invites us to seek our hearts' true home.

Congregation: Let us journey in faith, eager to follow where God leads.

Leader: The God of Love has sent the Spirit that we may travel in safety.

Congregation: Let us give thanks for the gifts of guidance and assurance.

Leader: The God of Mercy lifts us up when we stumble along the way.

Congregation: Let us rely upon the loving arms that embrace us with acceptance and peace.

Leader: The God of Community calls us to share our gifts and our journey with others.

All: Let us together lift our hearts and voices in praise and thanksgiving. Amen.

❧

Leader: As the Lord was present in the wilderness, guiding and guarding his beloved children, so God is present with us here.

Congregation: We rejoice in the presence of the Lord.

Leader: As the Lord blessed the people of Israel with refreshing water drawn from the rock, so may we find refreshment from the Rock of Our Salvation.

Congregation: We rejoice in the presence of the Lord.

Leader: The Israelites' faith was strengthened by their shared witness of God's loving providence. So may our faith be fortified by the Word of God in the fellowship of the church.

Congregation: We rejoice in the presence of the Lord.

All: Let us come into God's presence with gratitude and praise. Amen.

❧

Leader: Come into the house of the Lord.

Congregation: We come with our hearts full of thanks and praise.

Leader: Come into the house of the Lord.

Congregation:	We come with our petitions and our offerings.
Leader:	Come into the house of the Lord.
Congregation:	We come as needy children and willing servants.
Leader:	Come into the house of the Lord.
Congregation:	We come to worship the One who gathers us in and sends us out.
All:	Let us worship God. Amen.

∂℘

Leader:	Jesus, even as you fed the people beside the Sea of Galilee, feed us who hunger for your truth.
Congregation:	We gather to hear your Word.
Leader:	Jesus, even as you turned a young boy's meager provisions into a gift for many, so too may you bless others with the offerings we bring.
Congregation:	We gather to give thanks and to share what you have given us.
Leader:	Jesus, even as the people on the mountain proclaimed, "This is indeed the prophet who is to come into the world," inspire us with a knowledge of who you are and give us the courage to declare it.
Congregation:	We gather to bear witness and to sing our praises to you.
Leader:	We gather to worship our Teacher and Provider.
All:	Let us worship God. Amen.

∂℘

Leader:	The season of spring brings renewal to the earth.
Congregation:	Renew in us, O God, our commitment to love and serve you.
Leader:	Birds sing.

Congregation: Let us lift our voices in hymns of thanksgiving.

Leader: Flowers bloom.

Congregation: Let faith blossom anew.

Leader: Brooks babble and rivers swell their banks.

Congregation: Let us pray without ceasing; let our praises flow in abundance.

All: Let us worship the Creator, Sustainer, and Renewer of Life. Amen.

ॐ

Leader: We worship our Creator, Yahweh, Elohim, the Great "I AM."

Congregation: O Lord, our Sovereign, how majestic is your name in all the earth.

Leader: We worship the Savior, the Christ, Emmanuel, our Redeemer.

Congregation: O Lord, our Sovereign, how majestic is your name in all the earth.

Leader: We worship the Holy Spirit, the Advocate, the Breath of Life.

Congregation: O Lord, our Sovereign, how majestic is your name in all the earth.

Leader: We worship the triune God.

All: O Lord, our Sovereign, how majestic is your name in all the earth. Amen.

ॐ

Leader: We gather, remembering a God who made us and breathed life into us and who calls us "children." To our Creator, we give thanks and praise.

Congregation: We worship you, O God.

Leader: We gather, celebrating a God who brings healing and instruction, feeds us with the bread of life, and pours out salvation and eternal love. To our Savior, we give thanks and praise.

Congregation: We worship you, O God.

Leader: We gather, relying on a God who moves among us and provides understanding, sustains faith, and inspires hope. To our Advocate, we give thanks and praise.

Congregation: We worship you, O God.

All: Let us give thanks and praise; let us worship God. Amen.

❧

Leader: Creator God, even as you paint the trees of autumn, color our lives in ways that glorify you.

Congregation: We want to be changed by you, O God.

Leader: God of Salvation, even as you send the birds to warmer, safer dwelling places, keep us free from harm and help us to find our perfect home.

Congregation: We want to find rest and peace with you, O God.

Leader: Spirit of Hope, even as you promise today's barren trees new life in tomorrow's spring, fill us with the knowledge that we too will know rebirth in you.

Congregation: We want to claim your promise of a new day, O God.

Leader: In this season of change and beauty, let us recognize you, O Creator, Savior, and Sustainer, and let us respond with praise and love.

All: We come before you, O God, in worship. Amen.

❧

Leader:	In faith, the Israelites passed through the Red Sea as if it were dry land.
Congregation:	We pray, O God, for the faith to walk with assurance the paths you have prepared for us.
Leader:	In faith, the armies of Israel felled the walls of Jericho and claimed victory.
Congregation:	We pray, O God, for the strength to tear down the walls that separate us from you and from our brothers and sisters. Give us victory over doubt and hate.
Leader:	In faith, a cloud of ancestors calls us to persevere and to look to Jesus, who perfects our faith.
Congregation:	We pray, O God, for the wisdom to follow our Savior's example of love, grace, and endurance.
Leader:	In faith, we enter this place of worship, believing there is One who hears our prayers, forgives our sins, and is worthy of our adoration.
All:	Let us praise and worship God together in faith. Amen.

⁂

Leader:	We come to worship the God of Creation.
Congregation:	Make us good stewards of your abundant gifts, O God.
Leader:	We come to worship the God of Salvation.
Congregation:	Save us, O God, from all that destroys life and love.
Leader:	We come to worship the God of Inspiration.
Congregation:	O God, open our minds and our hearts to deeper meanings.
Leader:	We come to worship in hope and in faith.

Congregation:	We bring with us our need for healing and forgiveness.
Leader:	We come bearing gifts to lay at God's feet.
Congregation:	We come ready to receive and ready to serve.
Leader:	O God, take us as we are and mold us into what you would have us be.
All:	We offer ourselves to God in worship. Amen.

ॐ

Leader:	We gather here with hearts grateful for the beauty of nature, the wonder of life, and the love that unites us.
Congregation:	We give thanks and praise to the Creator.
Leader:	We gather here with hearts grateful for the gift of good news, the grace of salvation, the joy of resurrected life.
Congregation:	We give thanks and praise to the Redeemer.
Leader:	We gather here with hearts grateful for encouragement, and hope, and healing.
Congregation:	We give thanks and praise to the Comforter.
All:	Let us give thanks and praise; let us worship God.

ॐ

Leader:	We gather to ask your blessing, O God.
Congregation:	We are hungry for righteousness and longing for peace.
Leader:	We gather to hear your Word and to learn your ways.
Congregation:	We are grateful for redemptive teachings born of your love.
Leader:	We gather with the hope that we may bless others.

Congregation: We pray for purified hearts and for the courage to be faithful servants.

All: Let us praise and worship the God by whom we are blessed.

❧

Leader: God invites us to gather as beloved children, called and blessed.

Congregation: We gather to worship and praise our Creator.

Leader: Jesus invites us to break bread and to share the cup of salvation.

Congregation: We gather to worship and praise our Redeemer.

Leader: The Spirit invites us to receive and to respond to the message of abiding love.

Congregation: We gather to worship and praise our Intercessor.

All: Let us together worship and praise God.

❧

Leader: Come into this sacred place and open yourselves to Wisdom.

Congregation: We come, longing to hear the message of God.

Leader: Come into this sacred place and prepare to receive gracious gifts.

Congregation: We come, longing for the bread of salvation and the cup of blessing.

Leader: Come into this sacred place with hands ready to serve.

Congregation: We come, longing to offer our time and our gifts to God.

Leader: Come into this sacred place, ready to be challenged and changed.

Congregation: We come, longing to be all God has called us to be.

Leader:	Come into this sacred place, with faith and hope.
All:	We come to praise and worship God. Amen.

❧

Leader:	Even as Shiphrah and Puah chose righteousness over cowardice, may we prove to be courageous midwives in the birth of your New Creation.
Congregation:	God, help us to be faithful.
Leader:	Even as Miriam watched carefully to see what would happen to her brother, may we keep our eyes open for opportunities to serve your beloved children.
Congregation:	God, help us to be compassionate.
Leader:	Even as Pharaoh's daughter opened her heart and her home to one of the least of these, may we show hospitality to strangers and to those who are in need.
Congregation:	God, help us to be nurturing and generous.
Leader:	God, even as these women have shown forth your will and your ways, help us to become examples of what it means to live in covenant with you, that you may be glorified.
All:	Let us dedicate our lives to God, who is worthy of worship and praise. Amen.

❧

Leader:	We gather as God's own:
Congregation:	wanderers and wonderers,
Leader:	hungry for good news,
Congregation:	thirsting for renewal.
Leader:	We hold out our hands;
Congregation:	we lift up our hearts;

Leader:	we give praise and thanks to the One who made us, claims us, and encourages us.
All:	Let us worship and give thanks to our Creator, Redeemer, and Guide.

࣓

Leader:	God's house is a place of welcome;
Congregation:	may all who enter here find warm acceptance.
Leader:	God's house is a place of inspiration;
Congregation:	may all who enter here find deeper meaning.
Leader:	God's house is a place of generosity;
Congregation:	may all who enter here find ways to share their gifts.
Leader:	God's house is a place of prayer;
Congregation:	may all who enter here find the faith to call on God.
Leader:	God's house is a place of worship;
All:	may all who enter here give glory to God. Amen.

࣓

Leader:	We gather in the presence of God,
Congregation:	to pray and to praise
Leader:	in word, song, and deed;
Congregation:	to listen, and to learn,
Leader:	and to share Christ's good news!
Congregation:	We bow our heads,
Leader:	we raise our voices,
Congregation:	the Spirit guides, grace abounds,
Leader:	life is renewed, faith is restored, and gratitude grows.
All:	Let us worship our awesome God. Amen.

For Christmas Eve or Day

Leader: As Mary conformed her will to God's, may we too live lives obedient to God's call.

Congregation: We come as faithful servants.

Leader: As Joseph put aside his fears to accept angelic counsel, let us put God's plans before our own.

Congregation: We come as faithful listeners.

Leader: As the shepherds followed the star to Bethlehem, let us follow God's light in the darkness of our world.

Congregation: We come as faithful seekers.

Leader: As the heavenly hosts sang of his glory, let us sing in praise and in wonder.

Congregation: We come as faithful worshipers.

Leader: O come, all ye faithful.

All: Come, let us adore Christ the Lord.

❧

Leader: Look! In the darkness of a winter's night, there is One who shines the light of God's hope through the shadow of sorrow.

Congregation: Come, Messiah, Bringer of Hope, light our darkness.

Leader: Listen! Above the sobs of the oppressed and the threats of the warmongers comes the voice of the One whom the prophets foretold.

Congregation: Sing to your people, Prince of Peace, the song that silences hatred's furious raging.

Leader: Breathe deeply! Despite the pollution that proclaims our sin, there is yet the essence of eternal joy emanating from the holiest reservoir, the untainted heart of heaven's child.

Congregation:	Grace us, sweet Jesus, with the fragrant perfume of joyful renewal and holy redemption.
Leader:	Taste the goodness! There is One who forgives our wicked appetites and offers to feed those who hunger for righteousness and to satisfy those who thirst for justice.
Congregation:	O God, who is with us, fill us with your unconditional love that sustains and nourishes.
All:	Wonderful Counselor, enter our hearts and teach us the ways of hope, peace, joy, and love; walk with us to the manger and help us to find and claim the blessed gift of you. Amen.

For Palm Sunday

Leader:	As people gathered in Jerusalem singing your praises and preparing your way, so we, your people, gather today.
Congregation:	Write your desires on our hearts; let us too bring what is needed, share what we can, and lift you up.
Leader:	Send your Spirit to remind us of your deeds of power, so that we might declare with generations of faithful believers, "Blessed is the king who comes in the name of the Lord."
All:	Amen.

For Maundy Thursday

Leader:	Jesus, even as your disciples gathered for the Passover meal centuries ago to remember God's beneficence in the fulfillment of divine promises, so too are we here to remember.

Congregation:	We ask that as we gather in your name, you would be here with us.
Leader:	As we break bread, share the cup, and tell of your sacrifice of love, inspire and empower us.
Congregation:	Give us the faith and courage to respond in bold and meaningful ways to your commandment that we love one another as you have loved us, so that you may be glorified.
All:	Let us remember and worship the God of our salvation. Amen.

For Easter

Leader:	Like the women at the tomb, we have come to seek Jesus.
Congregation:	O God, roll away that which hinders our perception of Christ's victory over death.
Leader:	Like Mary Magdalene, when we feel confused or uncertain, may we faithfully continue to ask questions.
Congregation:	And may we too hear Christ calling us by name and telling us to remind others of his words.
Leader:	Like the angels, may we declare with confidence the good news of this day: "He has risen."
Congregation:	He has risen, indeed.
All:	Let us praise and worship our risen Lord. Amen.

3

Good for the Soul

Confessional Prayers

If we confess our sins, he who is faithful and just will forgive us our sins and cleanse us from all unrighteousness.

—1 JOHN 1:9

THESE CALLS TO CONFESSION and Prayers of Confession invite the congregation to reflect on the many ways we who call ourselves God's children fail to obey God's commandments, thereby destroying Creation and damaging our relationships both with God and with one another. Each prayer includes specific offenses that we may claim individually and corporately and concludes with a request for God's forgiveness and assistance in amending our ways so that, by grace through Christ, we may enjoy the hope of renewal. Prayers for specific Sundays of the liturgical year may be found after the Prayers for Ordinary Time.

Prayers for Ordinary Time

Call to Confession

Leader: In Matt 3:2, John the Baptist enjoins us, "Repent for the kingdom of heaven has come near." And we are aware of the need to change our ways and to turn to God to ask for forgiveness. Therefore, let us pray together the Prayer of Confession.

Prayer of Confession

All: God of Grace, we confess that we have not borne good fruit. Our pride has brought forth resentment; our anger has brought forth division; our deceit has brought forth distrust; our faithlessness has brought forth fear. We are sorry for the many ways we have grown apart from you. Do not, in return, cut us off but by your grace forgive us and cultivate in us the desire for the health and strength you alone provide. Help us to grow in ways that glorify you. In Jesus's name we pray. Amen.

Call to Confession

Leader: Jesus calls followers, giving new identities and showing new directions and possibilities. We have heard Christ's call; but we know that our response has not always been sincere or wholehearted. Let us pray together that God will help us to see those places where our attitudes and behaviors interfere with our discipleship. Let us invite Christ to enter our hearts anew so that we may be emboldened to do justice, to love kindness, and to walk humbly with our God.

Prayer of Confession

All: Gracious God, you sent Jesus, the Messiah, to live among us so that we might witness the depth of your love, experience the breadth of your grace, and share the heightened hope that the gift of renewed life inspires. We are grateful that, despite our fears and doubts, you invite us into partnership with you in the fulfillment of your divine plan. Throughout time, you have gifted your people and called us to minister in your name. But we confess that we have not always used our gifts in ways that glorify you. Grant that we may respond faithfully to your invitation to serve. Give us ears to hear your call, eyes to see the places where "our deep gladness and the world's deep hunger meet,"[1] and mouths ready to answer, "Here I am." Loving God, by the power of the Holy Spirit sent by Christ our Savior, fill our minds with the wisdom to understand your will, and fill our hearts with the courage to follow where you lead. We pray in Jesus's holy name. Amen.

Call to Confession

Leader: Friends, we have been blessed by the Spirit of God with gifts for the common good. But we often use our gifts inappropriately, and we envy the gifts of others. Our sinfulness is an affront to God, yet God mercifully forgives us when we confess our sin in Jesus's name. Therefore, let us pray together the Prayer of Confession.

Prayer of Confession

Leader: Gracious God, to some you have given the Spirit and utterance of wisdom and to others the utterance of knowledge.

1. Frederick Buechner, *Wishful Thinking: A Seeker's ABC* (New York: HarperCollins, 1993) 119.

Congregation: Forgive us when we speak in foolish and ignorant ways and deny the truth and understanding your Spirit brings.

Leader: Creator, to some you have given the gift of faith.

Congregation: Forgive us when we put our trust in false gods and do not place our lives in your loving hands.

Leader: Author of Life, to some you have given the gifts of healing; to others the gifts of miracles and prophecy, or the discernment of spirits or tongues.

Congregation: Forgive us when we neglect the sick and hurting people of our world, when we question the power of prayer, and when we fail to share the messages you write on our hearts or the good news you have given us to deliver.

Leader: Forgive us when we deny what we cannot explain and when we waste your good gifts in ways that renounce your grace and power in our lives.

All: Help us to trust your Holy Spirit and to declare in the language of love, "Jesus is Lord!"

Call to Confession

Leader: Christ came to proclaim a message of peace and love and to cast out evil. We are called to do the same, but we know that we often fail to act as faithful disciples to our Lord and Savior. Yet we also know that when we ask for forgiveness in Christ's name, God is merciful. Therefore, let us pray together the Prayer of Confession.

Prayer of Confession

All: Loving God, we confess that we have strayed from the paths of righteousness. We have not followed in the footsteps of Jesus. Christ tended the sick and showed compassion to those who suffered, but we fail to provide loving care to those who are hurting and in need. Jesus set aside the distractions of the day to speak to you and to seek your guidance, but we are caught up in the demands of this world and we don't find time to call upon you. Forgive us when we disobey you and when we ignore you. Restore us to your ways and your will. We pray in Jesus's holy name. Amen.

Call to Confession

Leader: Jesus calls us to hear God's Word and to act upon it faithfully. Yet we know that we often fail to act in ways that say we have heard; we know how often we are foolish and careless. But we also know that when we humbly ask, God forgives our sins and restores us to grace. Therefore, let us pray together the Prayer of Confession.

Prayer of Confession

All: Gracious God, you have given us a firm foundation on which to build our lives. But we confess that we find ourselves falling into the mire of sin. We do not turn to you when the storms of life come but struggle on our own, weighted in shame and drowning in sorrow. We rain down curses upon our neighbors and are caught in currents of stubbornness and pride. Forgive us and rescue us from ourselves; restore us to the Rock of Our Salvation. This we pray in Jesus's name. Amen.

Call to Confession

Leader: The Lord was displeased when the people asked Samuel to appoint for them a king to govern. Like them, we sometimes reject God's rule and find ourselves impoverished and enslaved. But God is gracious when we ask for forgiveness in Christ's name. Therefore, let us pray together the Prayer of Confession.

Prayer of Confession

All: Creator God, you are sovereign over all; but we are tempted to give our allegiance to things and people that lead us on destructive paths. We are ruled by the voice of commerce and the dictates of a hedonistic society. We ask that you will in mercy heal our hearts and help us to follow the voice of the Good Shepherd, who calls us to journey where peace and wholeness reside. In Jesus's name we pray. Amen.

Call to Confession

Leader: The prophet Amos tells us of God's great wrath when God's people behaved in unrighteous and impious ways, caring little for the poor and spending little time with God. We know that we today are worthy of God's wrath, for we too behave in ways that are unloving and sinful. Yet God redeems those who return to God in faith to pray for forgiveness. Therefore, let us confess our sins before the God of Redemption.

Prayer of Confession

All: Forgiving God, we confess that we have been neglectful of our duties as your children. Our priorities are not what they should be. Too often we hurry through worship and prayer, considering them an obligation instead of a privilege. We fail to set aside time in our schedules to read and reflect on your Word. We don't have a moment to consider and respond to the needs of our communities. We focus on money and what it can buy and on titles and the power they command. We are too busy to visit friends and family, to play with our children, or to share a meal with one another. And even as we put what is important last, we wonder at our own fatigue and lack of fulfillment. Help us to rearrange our lives in ways that are pleasing to you, O Holy One. Help us to put our faith not in things but in your abiding presence. Help us to notice those around us and to reach out in ways that say we have heard your Word and want to live according to your will. These things we pray in Jesus's name. Amen.

Call to Confession

Leader: In 1 John 1:8, we read, "If we say that we have no sin, we deceive ourselves, and the truth is not in us." Let us not deceive ourselves, but rather confess our sin to God and ask forgiveness in Christ's name, so that we may find mercy and wholeness.

Prayer of Confession

All: Lord, you are the Great Physician, but we do not come to you for healing. We deny your power, question your miracles, and seek to explain away the things that should fill us with wonder. We put our trust in the things of this world and then complain that we feel betrayed, broken, and unfulfilled. Forgive us our lack of faith and our vanity. Teach us to humble ourselves and to put our lives in your healing hands. Restore us to wholeness and send us forth to share the good news that you are a God who loves and who saves. In Jesus's name, we pray. Amen.

Call to Confession

Leader: In Rom 7:19, the Apostle Paul writes, "I do not do the good I want, but the evil I do not want is what I do." We know we are like the Apostle Paul in this regard, as we too find ourselves doing that which is evil in the sight of God. But we know that, even as Paul relied upon the grace of God, so too may we. Therefore, let us pray for God's grace as we confess our sins.

Prayer of Confession

All: Holy and Gracious God, we confess that we have not obeyed your Law and that we have not been led by your Word or your example. You call us to feed your sheep, but we close our ears to the cries of the hungry. You call us to share the good news, but we keep silent in a world that does not know you. You call us to make a joyful noise, but we whine and complain about what we do not have. And yet, we want to do the right thing. Forgive us our inability to resist temptation; forgive us our allegiance to the things of this world; and by the power of your Holy Spirit, let us hear anew your call to obedient discipleship. In Christ's name, we pray. Amen.

Call to Confession

Leader: Jesus taught us to pray, "Thy will be done," but we know that we often act in ways that are not in accordance with God's will. Jesus understood our human natures, and so he also taught us to pray, "Forgive us our debts." Let us therefore join together in the Prayer of Confession.

Prayer of Confession

All: O God, though Jesus taught us to call upon you, we confess that we forget to pray. And even when we do petition you, the language of our hearts does not correspond to the words of our mouths. We pray, "Hallowed be thy name," and then we use your name to curse our neighbors. We pray, "Thy kingdom come," but struggle to gain and maintain our own power. We pray for "daily bread" and then we hoard it. Forgive us our faithless contradictions and send your Spirit to instruct and transform us, so that the words of our mouths and the meditation of our hearts may be acceptable in your sight. Amen.

Call to Confession

Leader: In Rom 8:14, the Apostle Paul writes, "For all who are led by the Spirit of God are children of God." And though we are blessed to be called children of God, we know that we do not always follow where the Spirit leads. But we also know that God forgives our waywardness when we humbly confess our sins and ask for grace in Christ's holy name. Therefore, let us pray together the Prayer of Confession.

Prayer of Confession

All: Creator God, we hopefully await the day when your creation will be set free from the bondage of decay. And we know how often we contribute to the decay through our careless and thoughtless ways. We waste resources, we allow our minds and souls to be polluted by images and words that are hurtful and grotesque, and we fail to protect endangered plants and animals. Our selfish acts leave us fearful and guilt-ridden. Send your Spirit to intercede for us so that we may express to you the sorrow we feel for our transgressions and may know the healing power of your grace. We pray in Jesus's name. Amen.

Call to Confession

Leader: Though Jesus, the Great Physician, is ever-ready to bless our lives, we do not always respond as those who know his gracious healing. We are deaf when he calls us to serve and mute when we should proclaim our faith. Yet if we humbly ask forgiveness, our God is gracious. Therefore, let us pray together the Prayer of Confession.

Prayer of Confession

All: Giver of Life, we confess that we have failed to act as faithful children. We do not prayerfully come to you with our needs but instead strive to satisfy ourselves through greed and self-indulgence. We do not allow ourselves to be opened by your Word but instead twist your Word to our own ends. We do not zealously proclaim your power but instead keep quiet, despite your grace, for fear of what others may think or say. Forgive us our shabby discipleship and our crippling pride. Help us to reach out to you and to one another in truth and in love. In Christ's name, we pray. Amen.

Call to Confession

Leader: In the book of Romans, the Apostle Paul reminds us that we are children of the promise. But we know that we often live in ways that say, "We have not heard and believed God's promises." Yet God, in infinite mercy, forgives us when we humbly ask for grace. Therefore, let us pray together the Prayer of Confession.

Prayer of Confession

All: Redeemer God, you have been faithful to your children from generation to generation. Yet we who are heirs of your promise confess that we have not always responded in faith. You promise to guide and teach us, but we ignore the Scriptures and the example Jesus set. You promise to meet the physical needs of your people, but our greed undermines your providential work. You have promised to be with us always, but we do not seek your presence or call upon your name. Forgive us our unfaithfulness to your Word and your Way and mend the bonds that we have broken. We pray in Christ's name. Amen.

Call to Confession

Leader: Friends, we know that though we profess to be followers of Jesus and students of the Word, we act in ways that oppose Christ's leading and distort God's message. Our hypocrisy shames us. Yet when we confess our sin to God and ask for forgiveness in Christ's name, God is merciful. Therefore, let us pray together the Prayer of Confession.

Prayer of Confession

All: God of Grace, we come to you in need of forgiveness. We have distorted your teachings and misused your gifts. Your commandments should help us to create community, but we use your words to divide ourselves. We focus on those passages that serve us, and we overlook what seems too hard in your teachings. We are legalistic and judgmental, and our narrow-mindedness limits our expression of your expansive love. Forgive us when our mean interpretation impedes the healing and transforming power of the gospel. Open our hearts and minds to a more generous and honest understanding of your message and of your expectations of us as disciples. We pray in Jesus's name.

Call to Confession

Leader: Though Wisdom reaches out to us in reproof and makes known to us God's counsel, we continue to act in foolish ways and, in doing so, court disaster. But we find mercy when, in Jesus's name, we ask God to pardon our sinful folly. Therefore, let us pray together the Prayer of Confession.

Prayer of Confession[2]

All: Wisdom dictates that we should acquire knowledge of you, O God, and of your ways. But though you offer encouragement and guidance, we ignore your counsel. You call us and we turn away, mocking your teaching and rejecting your discipline. Forgive us our waywardness and our complacency and teach us to listen so that we may rest secure in the comfort of your abiding love and grace. In Jesus's name, we pray. Amen.

2 Based on Prov 1.

Call to Confession

Leader: Jesus declares, "What comes out of the mouth proceeds from the heart, and this is what defiles. For out of the heart come evil intentions, murder, adultery, fornication, theft, false witness, slander" (Matt 15:19). We know that too often our mouths and our hearts are full of that which defiles and offends. We are in need of God's restorative mercy and healing grace. Therefore, let us pray together the Prayer of Confession.

Prayer of Confession

All: Gracious God, we know how often we are guilty of foul language, gossip, mean words, and petty accusations. We know that our hearts are impure, that they harbor bitterness and greed. We ignore the cries of those who are suffering and let our prejudices overrule your call to be charitable. Forgive our hypocrisy when we declare ourselves to be followers of Christ even though our actions do not bear witness to your good news. Forgive us when we make idols of tradition and of human standards and fail to honor Christ's teachings and your commandments. Heal our hearts so that they may become sources of good intentions, fidelity, generosity, truth, and peace. In Jesus's name, we pray.

Call to Confession

Leader: Hebrews 5:9 tells us that Jesus is the source of salvation for all who obey him. But we are not obedient. We stray from the paths of righteousness and vainly go our own sinful ways. But God, in mercy, forgives us when we confess our sinfulness. Therefore, let us pray together the Prayer of Confession.

Prayer of Confession

All: God of Grace, you sent Jesus to be the seed for the fruits of peace, love, truth, and life. Jesus calls us to be his servants and to follow him; but we confess that we have not acted as followers of Jesus. What we plant does not produce a harvest pleasing to you. We sow seeds of distrust, fear, greed and hate and bring forth cynicism, prejudice, injustice, and war. Forgive us when we choose the temporal things of this world over the eternal joys you offer through the gift of your Beloved. Make us good and faithful servants. In Jesus's name, we pray. Amen.

Call to Confession

Leader: Though Jesus tells us that the greatest commandment is to "love the Lord your God with all your heart and soul and mind, and your neighbor as yourself" (Matt 22:37–39), we know that we often act in unloving ways. Yet we also know that God is gracious to those who humbly seek forgiveness. Therefore, let us pray together the Prayer of Confession.

Prayer of Confession

All: God of Our Lives, we confess that we have not obeyed your law of love. We stray from the paths of righteousness and wander in willfulness. We quarrel among ourselves and forget the teachings of those who have borne the torch of faith before us. Forgive us, O Holy One, and restore us to your ways so that we might reach out to others to share your goodness, your peace, and your love. Even as you are continually reforming your church, reform each one of us so that together we may truly become the church you call us to be, caring so deeply for your children that we "are determined to share . . . not only the gospel of God but also our own selves." (1 Thes 2:8) In Jesus's name, we pray. Amen.

Call to Confession

Leader: We know that as members of the Body of Christ, we are called to be a dwelling place for God. Yet too often we house resentment and disunity instead of the love and grace of the One who calls us together. But we know that when we ask forgiveness for being less than what God calls us to be, God is merciful. Therefore, let us pray together the Prayer of Confession.

Prayer of Confession

All: Shepherd God, we know that you have gathered us together and taught us your lessons of truth and hope so that we may know peace and healing and share them with others. But too often we live according to our own shameful standards. We are envious of those who have more and contemptuous of those who have less. We take more than our fair share and neglect the impoverished among us. Our thoughtlessness and greed create animosity and bitterness among your children. Our shortsightedness diminishes resources and depletes what you have prepared for future generations. Forgive us when we divide ourselves in foolish ways; remind us that our true happiness will only be found in loving one another as you love. In Christ's name, we pray.

Call to Confession

Leader: In Phil 3:13–14, the Apostle Paul seeks to forget what lies behind and to strain toward what lies ahead: the heavenly call of God in Christ Jesus. This should be our pursuit too, but our efforts to "press on toward the goal" are often halfhearted. Yet we know that if we humbly call upon God and ask forgiveness for our waywardness, God will hear and be gracious to us. Therefore, let us pray together the Prayer of Confession.

Prayer of Confession

All: Merciful God, we confess that we have put our faith in the things of this world. We hold fast to our possessions and forget your call to share what we have with one another. We get caught up in the pleasure of the moment, as though the future will hold no consequences. We know that we should strive to become like Christ, but instead we imitate pop idols and celebrities. Forgive us when we get off course, when we slow our efforts, when we are immature and shortsighted. Help us to keep the goal before us and be with us in our striving so that we may hold fast to what we have attained and enjoy your presence forever. In Christ's holy name, we pray. Amen.

For the Baptism of the Lord Sunday

Call to Confession

Leader: Friends, in Christ we are baptized with water and the Spirit; thus, we are freed from sin and offered new life. But we fail to cherish Christ's gift and turn, time and again, to old, fruitless ways. Yet if we confess our sin, God is gracious and reaches out to us with a blessed renewal of covenantal life. Therefore, let us pray together the Prayer of Confession.

Prayer of Confession

All: God of Grace, though our baptisms unite us with you and one another, we confess that there is division among us. We fight over theological understandings and bicker about worship styles. We separate ourselves from you by failing to keep your laws or to do what Jesus taught us. We fail to make disciples, to welcome the stranger, to feed the hungry. We do not pursue justice but make self-serving choices of convenience instead. Forgive us our disunity and disloyalty. Help us to be born again to lives of love and obedience. We pray in Jesus's name. Amen.

Or

Prayer of Confession

All: Creator God, you made us, baptized us with the Holy Spirit, and claimed us as your children. But we confess that we have not lived up to the promise of your anointing. We do not follow Christ's example of love and peace. We quarrel with our neighbors and among ourselves. We amass weapons and study war. We distrust those who do not look like us or speak our language. We ignore your commandments and your commission. Forgive us when we forget you and your Word. Cleanse us once more and fill us with your Spirit of Renewal so that we may return to the light of your love and grace. Help us to remember we belong to you. We pray in Christ's name. Amen.

For Transfiguration Sunday

Call to Confession

Leader: Through the prophet Moses, God has given us a clear understanding of who and what we are to be as covenant people. Yet we continue to behave as though we are ignorant of God's laws. But God forgives us when we confess our transgressions and offers us gracious renewal. Therefore, let us confess our sin to God. Please join in the Prayer of Confession.

Prayer of Confession

All: Holy God, you call us to places of greater perspective, yet we cling to our jaded views. You want us to hear the voice of heaven, but we listen instead to the call of temptation. We have glimpsed your glory, but our lives do not reflect an awareness of who you are. Forgive us when we, like Peter, offer you huts when you want us to be temples. Transfigure us, O God, so that we might be restored to your image and likeness through Christ our Lord. Amen.

For the Start of the Lenten Season

Call to Confession

Leader: From the beginning of time, the Creator has cautioned against that which would lead to disillusionment and fear. Yet we have chosen to ignore God's words and have listened instead to distorted truths and empty promises. Our foolish choices have brought us only sorrow and alienation. But ours is a God of mercy who continually calls wayward children home and who runs to meet us when we turn from our sinful paths, aware of our need for forgiveness. Therefore, let us together pray for restoration. Please join in the Prayer of Confession.

Prayer of Confession

All: God of Eternal Truth, Jesus reminds us that we do not live by bread alone but by every word that comes from your mouth; nevertheless, we confess that we allow our appetites and our need for immediate gratification to lead us into temptation. Jesus teaches us that we should not put you to the test, but we confess that we expect you to perform according to our desires and our human understanding of your promises. Jesus worshipped and served only you, but we confess that we too often ignore you in the pursuit of earthly riches and titles. Forgive us and, in this season of reflection and repentance, help us to find the strength and courage to renounce the power of evil in our lives and in our world. We pray in Jesus's name. Amen.

For Palm Sunday

Call to Confession

Leader: The Apostle Paul enjoins us to "work out [o]ur own salvation with fear and trembling" (Phil 2:12). But we know that we often ignore this advice and behave arrogantly instead, preferring our own ways to God's. Yet we also know that if we come before God with repentant hearts and confess our waywardness, we will find forgiveness. Therefore, let us confess our sin to God.

Prayer of Confession

All: Gracious God, we confess that we have been more silent than stones. We should sing with gratitude for your presence among us, but instead we complain about what we do not have. Like those who threw down their cloaks, we should lay down what we have for your use, but instead we make gods of our possessions. We should, as your disciples, prepare a path for you, but by our sinful ways we become stumbling blocks that hinder your Word's progress. Forgive us our false witness and our greed. Teach us to celebrate the gift of Jesus; teach us, your children, to shout "Hosanna!"

Or

Prayer of Confession

Leader: God of Grace, forgive us; for we confess that we have been neither humble nor obedient.

Congregation: We declare, "Jesus is Lord," but we do not let Christ rule our lives and we do not follow where Christ leads.

Leader: He emptied himself; we puff ourselves up.

Congregation: He took the form of a slave; we serve only ourselves.

Leader: He was prepared to die to glorify you; we live for our own glory and reward.

Congregation: Forgive us our hypocrisy and faithlessness and transform us so that the same mind that was in Christ may be in us.

All: Amen.

For Holy Week

Call to Confession

Leader: The Apostle Paul enjoins us to "Stand firm in the Lord." But we know how often our God "is the belly" and our minds "set on Earthly things" (Phil 3:19).

Therefore, let us pray together the Prayer of Confession.

Prayer of Confession

All: Jesus, you would have gathered your people as a mother hen gathers her chicks. But we have always been a stubborn race. Our willfulness nailed you to a cross. Your mother wept for you, even as you wept for us—so many tears, so much pain. And still, we have not learned to let you hold us. Still we wander, lost and afraid, and know not what we do. Forgive us! Teach us to be obedient, grateful children. Teach us to let you enfold us in the loving arms that are our true home. Amen.

Call to Confession

Leader: Friends, though Jesus wants to free us from the bonds of sin and the pain it brings, we do not always welcome his help. We continue to turn deaf ears to wisdom and to ignore God's commandments. We need to ask forgiveness for our waywardness. Let us pray together the Prayer of Confession.

Prayer of Confession

All: Jesus, like the thief beside you, I too want to be remembered. I know that I am deserving only of condemnation, but in your sacrifice is my hope of paradise. Cleanse me and keep me listening for that still, small voice that calls me to eternal peace with you. Amen.

Or

Prayer of Confession

All: Savior, let me proclaim in my heart and in the life I live that I know you are the Son of God, the Messiah. Forgive me when my sinfulness mocks you in ways that are as painful as the jeers of those who crucified you. May I never deny you or the transforming power of your sacrifice and grace. Make my words and deeds befit One who is called to serve the Most High. Amen.

Or

Prayer for Transformation

Leader: Lord, how you long to make us clean, to wash away the stain of sin and the dust of the wayward paths we wander.

Congregation: But we, like Peter, fail to understand the meaning of your servant ministry. Help us to hear your words with greater clarity and to witness your works with greater appreciation.

Leader: Lord, how you long to teach us love, to be our example of obedience to the greatest commandment.

Congregation: But we betray you and deny your teaching. We let prejudice guide us and we let wrath consume us. We wage war and worship wealth and power.

Leader: Lord, how you suffer for our transgressions; our ignorance and obstinacy are nails and thorns.

Congregation: Forgive us our trespasses and deliver us from evil, so that you may be glorified and your kingdom may come. In Jesus's name, we pray. Amen.

For Easter Sunday

Call to Confession

Leader: In Phil 2:12, the Apostle Paul reminds us of the good news through which we have been saved, if we hold firmly to the message that was proclaimed to us. But we know we often let go of the good news and embrace that which is not of God. Yet we also know that God shows mercy when we repent and seek forgiveness. Therefore, let us pray together the Prayer of Confession.

Prayer of Confession

Jesus, you have offered us the gift of eternal life but so often we live only for today. When it serves us to do so, we deny you; when we're faced with the consequences of our own actions, we take out our anger on you; when you call us to share your message, our response is often silence. Forgive us our shortsightedness, our recalcitrance, and our unwillingness to serve. Help us to remember it is only by your grace that we are reborn and restored to right relationship with God. Help us to be grateful recipients and bearers of your good news. Amen.

For Pentecost Sunday

Call to Confession

Leader: Jesus sent the Spirit to remind us of all that he had taught us. Yet we know how often we fail to heed the Spirit's call to obey Christ's lessons. But we also know that when we humbly confess our stubbornness and sinfulness, God graciously forgives us. Therefore, let us pray together the Prayer of Confession.

Prayer of Confession

All: Almighty God, you poured your Spirit upon the gathered disciples, creating bold tongues, open ears, and a new community of faith. We confess that we hold back the force of your Spirit among us. We do not listen for your word of grace, speak the good news of your love, or live as a people made one in Christ. Have mercy on us, O God: transform our timid lives by the power of your Spirit and fill us with a flaming desire to be your faithful people as we do your will for the sake of Jesus Christ our Lord, in whose name we pray. Amen.

For World Communion Sunday

Call to Confession

Leader: God has given the people commandments by which we may live lives that are pleasing to God and honorable among God's children. But we confess that we have disobeyed and ignored God's words. Despite our sinfulness, God continues to walk beside us and to offer forgiveness and mercy to those who ask in the name of Jesus. Therefore, let us pray for grace in Christ's holy name.

Prayer of Confession

All: God, you call us to the table of plenty and invite us to be a family of peace. Yet we confess that we refuse what you have prepared for us. We treat some of your children as enemies and will not sit beside them at the table. We act as though you will not provide enough for all of us; we forget that with you a loaf of bread becomes a banquet for multitudes. We stockpile what we call our own and let others do without what they need. And worse, we teach our children our evil ways so that our spitefulness and greed multiply daily. Remind us that you love us all and that you call us all to love one another. In the poverty of others, let us see our need to share; in the cries of our neighbors, let us hear your call to comfort your people; in the trembling hand of the fearful, let us see the shakiness of our own small faith so that we may reach out with kindness instead of disdain. Help us to seek blessed communion with you. We pray in the name of Jesus Christ, our Savior. Amen.

For Christ the King Sunday

Call to Confession

Leader: Jesus says that, if we belong to the truth, we will listen to his voice. But we know how often we do not listen or obey. We fail to live truthfully. Yet we also know that when we confess our sins to God prayerfully in Jesus's name, we are led from the darkness of our deceit and are restored to righteousness. Therefore, let us pray together the Prayer of Confession.

Prayer of Confession

All: Gracious God, you sent Jesus to embody your Word, to reveal the meaning of that which the prophets declared, and to be known in the breaking of bread. Yet we confess that we fail to study your Word, we argue about prophets and what they say, and we break bread with little consideration as to its provider. But we know, O Holy One, that you are the provider of all good things, and we pray that you will forgive us our ignorance and our arrogance and cause us to confront ourselves. Grant us trust in your Word and pardon for our sins. We pray in Jesus's name. Amen.

For the Season of Advent

Call to Confession

Leader: In Rom 13:11, the Apostle Paul declares that it is now the moment to wake from sleep. But we know that we are not alert to the day of Christ's coming. We have been lazy and foolish disciples. But we also know that when we confess our sin to God in Jesus's name, God is merciful. Therefore, let us pray together the Prayer of Confession.

Prayer of Confession

All: Lord of Love, we confess that we have been sleepy disciples. We have not attended to your commandments or to your call. We are not alert to the cries of the needy; we fail to rise, and shine, and go forth bringing your good news. We should be joyous and expectant as we await Christ's coming, but we confess that we let the things of this world draw us into sin and despair. Forgive us our laziness and our apathy. Help us to hear anew the message of this season—that you "so loved" us. Help us to love you more. Wake us up, O God. In Jesus's name, we pray. Amen.

Call to Confession

Leader: In Jas 5:7 we read, "Be patient, therefore, beloved, until the coming of the Lord." But we are not patient people; we question God's timing and let our frustrations lead us into sin. But we know that when we ask God to forgive us in Jesus's name, we find mercy. Therefore, let us pray together the Prayer of Confession.

Prayer of Confession

All: Loving God, help us! In this season of Advent, we are reminded that we, like people in ancient times, should await the coming Messiah with confidence and hope. But we confess that we are anxious and faithless. We fill this time with hurry, and we worry more about presents wrapped in paper than we do about the gift of your Chosen One. We are so busy stringing lights on trees that we fail to look for the One who can truly light our darkness and bring healing to our stressful lives. Forgive us, open our blind eyes, and unstop our deaf ears so that our senses may be filled with the peace and beauty of Emmanuel, in whose name we pray. Amen.

Litany of Confession

Leader:	When our days are punctuated by angry words of hatred and ingratitude,
Congregation:	forgive us and grant us peace.
Leader:	When the pained cries of the oppressed grow louder around us because we have not shown compassion or love,
Congregation:	forgive us and grant us peace.
Leader:	When war's cacophony silences the sweet voices of children,
Congregation:	forgive us and grant us peace.

Leader: When we heed the call of commerce and ignore the cries from the manger,

Congregation: forgive us and grant us peace.

Leader: When the sinful noise of this world aggrieves you, Holy One, hear again the call from the cross, "Forgive them; they know not what they do,"[3] and, in mercy,

Congregation: forgive us and grant us peace.

Call to Confession

Leader: In Ps 80:18b, the psalmist writes, "give us life, and we will call on your name." But though God renews us, we neglect to thank God in the way we live our lives. We forget to call on God for direction but instead go our own sinful ways. Yet ours is a gracious God who saves us from ourselves and from our faithlessness. Let us then call upon God, asking forgiveness in Christ's name. Please join me in the Prayer of Confession.

Prayer of Confession

All: O God, we confess that though Jesus showed us the way to salvation, we have chosen paths of destruction. Unlike Joseph, who responded to your call with obedience and love, taking Mary for his wife, we have done what is easy and self-serving. We care more for our reputations than for the needs of your little ones. We judge others harshly but make excuses for our own callous behavior. Our selfishness makes enemies of our neighbors and threatens the peace and prosperity you offer. Forgive us, O God, and look upon us with mercy. "Restore us, O Lord God of hosts; let your face shine, that we may be saved" (Ps 80:19).

3 Luke 23:34.

For Christmas Eve

Call to Confession

Leader: Though Zechariah prophesies that the dawn from on high will guide our feet into the way of peace, we know that we frequently stray from the path that Christ illumines for us. Yet if we confess our waywardness, we will discover peace anew in the forgiveness that is Christ's gracious gift. Therefore, let us pray together the Prayer of Confession.

Prayer of Confession

Leader:	Loving God, you sent Jesus to lead us in the way that we should go. He came as a helpless child to a woman of lowly birth.
Congregation:	Yet we confess that we ignore the cries of the helpless and the poor.
Leader:	He lived a life of simplicity, reaching out to others to heal and to comfort.
Congregation:	Yet we confess that we seek wealth and power and that we put our own desires before the needs of others.
Leader:	He died that we might have eternal life.
Congregation:	Yet we confess that we lack the faith to embrace new life and that we set our sights on things that destroy our very souls.
All:	Forgive us, O God, when we wander in darkness and restore us to those paths that are radiant with the light of your loving guidance. We pray in the name of the One who came and is coming. Amen.

Prayer for Grace

Leader: The child born in the Bethlehem stall came that we might know what it is to live lives of love for God and one another. Then, as now, the world knew hatred, prejudice, and deceit. Then, as now, sin marred the beauty of God's creation. And so God sent a light to shine in the darkness, a light of grace to save us from evil and to bring the peace that surpasses all understanding. Please join me in the Litany of Grace, derived from Titus 2:11–14.

Litany of Grace

Leader: For the grace of God has appeared, bringing salvation to all.

Congregation: Lead us to grace and peace, O God.

Leader: This grace teaches us to renounce impiety and worldly passions and to live lives that are self-controlled, upright, and godly as we wait for the blessed hope and glorious appearing of our great God and Savior, Jesus Christ.

Congregation: Teach us to embrace the teachings of grace, O God, and to wait faithfully for Christ's return.

Leader: Christ gave himself for us that he might redeem us from all iniquity and purify for himself his own special people who are zealous for good deeds.

Congregation: Make us zealous for all that is holy and just in your eyes, O God. Help us to live lives that illustrate your boundless grace. Grant us forgiveness and peace. Amen.

For the Weeks After Christmas

Call to Confession

Leader: Jesus came into the world to be our light in the darkness. Yet we know that we often turn from the light and allow evil to overshadow goodness. But we also know that when we confess our sin and ask for grace, God hears and is merciful. Therefore, let us pray together the Prayer of Confession.

Prayer of Confession

All: God of Grace, we know that Jesus is close to your heart and that we may know you through him, and yet we do not turn to Christ or follow him faithfully. He was with you at Creation, bringing life; but we are guilty of destroying your Creation through greed and ignorance. He fed the multitudes, but we ignore the hungry. He worked to fulfill your law, but we break covenant with you and fail to keep your commandments. He died to save us, but we are unwilling to make those sacrifices that would bring nearer the world you intend for us. Forgive us when we choose darkness over light and falsehood over truth. Help us to live lives in imitation of Christ, by whom you are made known to us and in whose name we pray. Amen.

Call to Confession

Leader: In Isa 60:11b, the prophet tells us, "the Lord God will cause righteousness and praise to spring up before all the nations." But we know that we often forsake the paths of righteousness and neglect to give praise and glory to God. Yet we also know that when we confess our opposition to God's plan and ask God's forgiveness for our sins, God is merciful. Therefore, let us pray together the Prayer of Confession.

Prayer of Confession

All: God of Grace, you sent your Son to redeem us so that we might be called your children. But we confess that we have not acted in ways that say we belong to you. Our behavior declares we are slaves to the laws of fashion who bend to the demands of status and popularity. We ignore the needs of our sisters and brothers and disregard the promptings of the Holy Spirit, who calls us to become a family in Christ. Forgive us when we do not claim the inheritance that is ours. Restore us to right relationship with you and with one another. We pray in Jesus's holy name. Amen.

4

Joy by the Answer

Prayers of Response to the Word

*To make an apt answer is a joy to anyone, and a word in
season, how good it is!*

—Prov 15:23

Having heard God's word read and expounded, we give thanks
and ask that God will continue to increase our understanding and
our recognition of God's leading as we seek to live in ways that
convey our embrace of the good news. The prayers in this section
express gratitude and a desire to find the courage to live according
to the Word. They include litanies of response, offertory prayers,
prayers of the people, communion prayers, and charges and bene-
dictions .

Responses to the Message

A Call for Guidance

Leader: God, when I ignore your commandments and heed my own vain counsel,

Congregation: open my ears that I may hear.

Leader: God, when I fail to search for you, when I walk in darkness and stubbornly follow fruitless paths,

Congregation: open my eyes that I may see.

Leader: God, when I am silent in the face of others' need,

Congregation: teach me to cry out for justice, to speak a kind word, and to tell of your wondrous love.

All: God, use all of me to proclaim that Jesus lives and reigns forever. Amen.

Expressions of Gratitude

Leader: For the earthly ministry of Jesus, who taught with authority in truth and in love,

Congregation: we give you thanks, O God.

Leader: For the Holy Spirit who inspired the apostles and has guided your people from age to age,

Congregation: we give you thanks, O God.

Leader: For the saints and martyrs who lived and died spreading the good news with courage and faith,

Congregation: we give you thanks, O God.

Leader: For the missionaries and teachers who continue to encourage others to turn to you,

Congregation: we give you thanks, O God.

63

Leader: As we learn to be discerning students and witnesses to Christ, the fulfillment of your holy promises,

Congregation: we give you thanks, O God.

❧

Leader: O God, through your prophet Hosea, you promised to lure your people back to you.

Congregation: We are grateful for ears to hear your call.

Leader: We are exhorted by your servant David, to bless you for all you are and all you have done.

Congregation: We are grateful for voices to sing your praise.

Leader: The Apostle Paul reminds us that we are empowered by your Holy Spirit to minister to your people.

Congregation: We thank you for hands to do your work.

Leader: Jesus says, "No one puts new wine into old wineskins" (Mark 2:22).

Congregation: We thank you for making us new and for filling us with your unconditional love.

All: With all our hearts, for all our days, we will give you thanks, O God.

During Advent

In this season of hope, as we await your coming, awaken us to the many ways you reveal yourself to us. May we see you in the faces of all who are hungry; hear you in the cry of every child who pleads for love's embrace; touch you when we reach for the hands of the sick and the lonely; and know you in the joy that comes when we shake off the slumber of complacency and attend to your call to care for the hurting, the ignored, and the misguided. Help us, in this season of preparation, to search our hearts, to welcome holy mystery, to renew our commitment to you, and to serve as faithful followers, O Christ, our Light and our Lord. Amen.

During Easter Season

Gracious God, through your Word, we witness the steadfastness of your disciples who, through days of disdain and nights of imprisonment, held high your name and kept your commandments. May we, for whom you prayed, be faithful too, remembering always that love has made us one with you and with our Creator through the guidance of the Holy Spirit. We are grateful for the joy of your resurrection and for the knowledge that we too shall rise. May our lives reflect our gratitude. In Christ's name, we pray. Amen.

Prayers of the People—Intercessory Prayer

Leader: God, as your people, we are called to love and to pray for one another. We know that you hear and answer all our prayers according to your wisdom and will. We ask that you would give healing to those who suffer, comfort to those who mourn, peace to those who are troubled, direction to those who lead, and continued gladness to those who are celebrating your bountiful gifts. Be with us now as we silently lift up our personal joys and concerns. *(At the conclusion of a period of silence, the leader continues.)* Hear our prayer, O Lord, and let our cries come to you. In Jesus's name, we pray. Amen.

❧

Leader: This is the time in our service when we pray for one another. As I name various categories of joy and concern, I invite you to use the silences to lift up the names of those who are in need of prayer. You may do so aloud or in your hearts. Let us pray.

Loving God, we thank you that you are a God who comes beside us in the joys and sorrows of life, and who listens when we call on you. We are thankful for the blessings that we share—our families, our freedom, the fellowship of this congregation, and the beauty of your world—and we ask that you would help us to live lives that reflect our gratitude. We thank you for the joy we feel, and we pray for those who have reason to celebrate. *(Pause)* We thank you for our health, and we pray for those in need of healing. *(Pause)* We thank you for our safety, and we pray for those who are in harm's way. *(Pause)* We thank you for our loved ones, and we pray for those who are grieving the loss of those who are dear to them. *(Pause)* In our joys and in our sorrows, we know you are near and we pray to you with faith, in the name of Jesus Christ, who taught us to pray, saying: *(The Lord's Prayer is said)* Amen.

Prayers of Dedication for Offerings

We thank you, God, for the many gifts with which you have entrusted us. May these offerings go out into the world to preserve your glorious creation, to bless your beloved children, and to serve your divine plan. We pray in Jesus's holy name. Amen.

❧

May these, our gifts, affirm the life-giving, hope-building, justice-seeking truth that God is Love and that we are all God's children, called to serve and to share our blessings for God's glory in Christ's name. Amen.

❧

Loving God, as we await your coming, may these, our gifts, declare that we are impatient for the day when your justice reigns, your peace is known, and your love reaches every corner of Creation. Bless these offerings to your holy use. In Christ's name, we pray. Amen.

❧

Creator of All Good Things, may these gifts, given in gratitude, go out into the world to bear witness to the One who calls us to live as brothers and sisters. Use what we offer to bring greater unity and peace among your children. In Christ's name, we pray. Amen.

❧

Gracious God, may the gifts we present to you this day serve to comfort the grieving, empower the weak, and bring good news to the poor in spirit. Help us to share your blessings in ways that teach others of a God who lifts up the lowly, heals the hurting, and frees the oppressed. In Jesus's name, we pray. Amen.

❧

Loving God, may the gifts you have given to us and that we now return for your use bring the light of your transforming love to the dark and desperate places of our world, giving hope to the hurting and glory to you. In Jesus's name we pray. Amen.

❧

God of Grace, receive these gifts and bless them to be a means by which hatred is silenced, bigotry decried, and intolerance overcome, so that we may live kind and compassionate lives to your greater glory, through Christ our Lord. Amen.

❧

Merciful God, we are grateful that Jesus has conquered death and offers us the gift of eternal life. May these gifts that we return to you bring renewal to your hurting children and afford them a vision of changed lives. We pray in the name of the Holy One, the Christ. Amen.

❧

Generous God, we thank you for the gift of faith, and in faith we return these gifts to you so that they may bear witness to your good news, banish doubt, and restore hope to a world in need. This we pray in Jesus's name. Amen.

❧

Holy, healing God, many are your gifts to us: gifts of knowledge, food for our bodies and souls, and hope for the days to come. May the gifts we return to you serve to teach others of a God who is beneficent beyond all understanding. In Christ's name, we pray. Amen.

❧

Giver of All Good Gifts, we thank you for the lessons we learn through ancient histories, the parables Jesus told, the lives of your saints, and the whisperings of your Holy Spirit. May the gifts we give help others to learn of your abiding faith and boundless love. We pray in Jesus's name. Amen.

❧

Light of the World, take these, our gifts, and bless them that they may become instruments of your peace and love. May what we bring be pleasing in your sight and useful in the fulfillment of your divine plan. We pray in the name of your Beloved. Amen.

⁊⁊

God of Inspiration, bless these gifts that they may bring a ray of hope into the lives of those who know the darkness of despair. Use what we bring to make known the good news of your great love. We pray in Jesus's name. Amen.

⁊⁊

Author of Life, we are filled with joy each time we remember the wonderful gift you have given us in the Word that came to live among us. Receive these gifts as an expression of our gratitude and bless them that they may become a source of joy for others to your greater glory. We pray in Jesus's name. Amen.

⁊⁊

We thank you, God, for your many gifts to us. May our offerings help others to see and know you so that our world may be changed and that you may be glorified. In Christ's holy name, we pray. Amen.

⁊⁊

In gratitude, O Lord, we make our offerings of time, talent, and treasure. Take the gifts we bring and use them to promote peace, to banish bigotry, and to show forth your love and comfort to the lonely, the oppressed, the imprisoned, and the suffering. May what we offer serve a world in need and bring glory to you. In Jesus's name, we pray. Amen.

⁊⁊

Bringer of Hope and Peace, take these gifts and bless them so that they may bring joy to your children. Use them to share the good news of your great love so that others may know of the One who came and is coming, our Holy Savior, Jesus Christ, in whose name we pray. Amen.

ह०

Holy One, you turn water into wine. Take these, our humble offerings, and by your grace let them become agents of change so that
our world may become a more loving, peaceful, generous place; so
that your vision might be realized; and so that you may be glorified. Amen.

ह०

Loving God, we can scarcely begin to understand the incredible
gift to us of your Beloved. May the gifts we bring in gratitude to
you this day become a means by which your children may learn of
One who loves us even unto death. Amen.

On Easter

Generous God, we thank you for the gifts of this day: the gift of a
promise fulfilled, the gift of Christ's incomparable sacrifice, the gift
of eternal life. May these gifts that we return to you manifest our
gratitude and contribute to the furtherance of your divine plan so
that you may be glorified. In Jesus's name, we pray. Amen.

Prayers for the Celebration of the Lord's Supper

At the Start of the Communion Service

Celebrant: Lord, we your children are faint with grief.

Congregation: Feed us with the bread of divine comfort.

Celebrant: Lord, we your children are weak with doubt.

Congregation: Feed us with the bread of empowering faith.

Celebrant: Lord, we your children are hungry for wisdom.

Congregation: Fill us with the presence of your Holy Spirit and teach us to feed others too.

Celebrant: For you are the bread that came down from heaven.

All: You are the bread of eternal life. And we who share this bread will hunger no more. Amen.

‽

Celebrant: With the bread of life and the cup of blessing, by the hand of the Almighty, we are fed.

Congregation: With the bread of friendship and the cup of kindness, we feed others in Christ's name.

Celebrant: Come to the table of transformation, where simple gifts are made a feast.

Congregation: We come in awe; we leave grace-filled to share the joy of God's good news. Amen.

Prayers of Thanksgiving at the End of the Communion Service

Celebrant: In the breaking of the bread and the sharing of the cup, there is hope—

Congregation: —hope that we will all be seated one day at a table where greed has no place and where all are equal and at peace with one another.

Celebrant: We are grateful for glimpses of what will be.

Congregation: In our gratitude, may we do our part to love all of our brothers and sisters and to promote unity as together we seek to know God's will and to follow God's ways. We pray in Christ's holy name. Amen.

❧

Holy God, through your divine providence we have broken bread and shared the cup. May we, who have been strengthened by these gifts, go forth now to feed the hungering souls around us with your bountiful good news. Bless us so that the lives we lead in response to your grace may become an invitation to others to join us at the table of remembrance and hope. In Christ's name, we pray. Amen.

❧

Gracious and generous God, we have broken bread and shared the cup as a family of faithful followers. Strengthened by your nurturance, may we go forth to share good news, to show mercy and compassion, and to invite others to put their trust in the Beloved One, who died and rose that we might have life in abundance. In your holy name, we pray. Amen.

❧

God of Light and Love, by your generous hand we have been fed. Give us the grace to remember your commandment to feed your sheep until all the world has been nurtured and blessed. We pray in Jesus's name. Amen.

⁊

God of Love, we thank you for calling us to this table, and we ask that we, who have been fed bountifully, might share with others that which sustains and blesses us in the name of the Creator, and of the Christ, and of the Holy Spirit. Amen.

⁊

Thank you, God, for your presence here and for nourishing our souls with the bread and the cup. May we, who have been lovingly fed, feed others; may we, who have been shown grace, show grace to others; may we, who have been led to this table, invite others to the table where all are welcomed. In Jesus's name, we ask this. Amen.

On Easter

By your hand, Gracious God, we have been fed. In the joy of this Easter morning, as we celebrate Christ's resurrection, we have come to the table as witnesses to the power of love. We remember the sacrifice Christ made so that we might not know the bitterness of death. As we embrace the good news that eternal life is ours through the victory of our Lord and Savior, help us to find the means to share our joy and your gospel message with all we meet. In Christ's name, we pray. Amen.

Charges and Benedictions

As you depart, take with you the lessons of this day; go forth with renewed determination to live according to Christ's teachings and to share Christ's message of hope and love. And, in the days ahead, may God's peace abide with you through the grace of Christ and the power of the Holy Spirit. Amen.

⁊

Go forth now with grateful and willing hearts, eager to serve God and to share good news. And may the blessings of the Creator, the hope of the Redeemer, and the inspiration of the Holy Spirit be with you today and always. Amen.

అ

You have heard God's Word; now share the Word.

You have been shown grace; show grace to others.

You have given your tithes and offerings; continue to ask how you might best use what God has provided.

And, as you leave this place, may you take with you the love, hope, peace, and joy born of faith in God, the Creator, the Christ, and the Holy Spirit. Amen.

5

There Is a Season

Prayers for Holy Days and Special Occasions

*For everything there is a season, and a time
for every matter under heaven.*

—ECCL 3:1

HOLIDAYS, SCOUTING EVENTS, FAMILY celebrations, hospitaliza-
tions, military deployment—many are the seasons and occasions
that call for prayerful consideration and response. This chapter
addresses some of the many occasions when ministers and church
leaders are called upon to lift up in prayer the events and times that
affect the lives of congregations.

A Thanksgiving Prayer

Giver of All Good Things,

we thank you for the bounty of the harvest,

and we ask you to bless those who have no food.

We thank you for the warmth of our homes,

and we ask you to bless those who are homeless.

We thank you for our families and friends,

and we ask you to bless the lonely and bereft.

We thank you for the peace of our community,

and we ask you to bless those who live in places of unrest.

We thank you for all that is loving, and gracious, and hopeful in our lives,

and we ask you to bless those who know only hatred, disgrace, and despair.

We thank you for all your generous gifts,

and we ask that you help us to heed your call to give generously to others.

May we be ever-thankful for what we receive and ever-mindful of those who have less. Amen.

Prayer for the Women of the Church
A Mother's Day Prayer

Leader:	Loving God, as we celebrate motherhood this day, we give you thanks for all the women who have nurtured us:
Congregation:	mothers and grandmothers, aunts and friends, teachers and coaches, pastors and healers.
Leader:	We thank you for those who have raised us to know you and taught us to gratefully walk in your light.
Congregation:	We thank you for those who make cookies for bake sales, kiss away booboos, and sing silly songs,
Leader:	who read bedtime stories, drive daily carpools, and volunteer time in our churches and schools.
Congregation:	We thank you for those who rise early and work late, who are quick to give guidance and slow to condemn.
Leader:	We thank you for all the ways they have challenged us, hoping that we might become our best selves.
Congregation:	We pray you will bless them with courage and confidence, help them to know they are needed and loved,
Leader:	grant them renewal and rest when they weary, strengthen their faith, and walk with them each day.
Congregation:	And may those who have gone to rest in your arms know the joy of the words, "Well done, faithful servant." Their lives shaped our lives; their love is our guidepost.
All:	God bless all the women who bless all of us. Amen.

A Prayer for the Men of the Church
A Father's Day Prayer

Leader:	Creator God, we celebrate and give you thanks for the men of the church:
Women and Children:	for those who lead and for those who join committees;
Leader:	for those who teach and for those who attend Sunday school;
Women and Children:	for those who speak from the heart, boldly at the front of the church or silently in the pew;
Leader:	for those who pray, and for those who need our prayers.
Women and Children:	We thank you for the time, talent, and treasures they share.
Leader:	We thank you for painters and electricians, treasurers and clerks;
Women and Children:	for elders and deacons, pruners and plumbers;
Leader:	for greeters and storytellers, cooks and cleaners;
Women and Children:	for musicians and worship leaders;
Leader:	for devoted husbands, dedicated dads, and loving sons;
Women and Children:	for beloved uncles and godfathers;
Leader:	for cousins, and classmates, and friends.
Women and Children:	We pray for the strong and the weak,

Leader:	the hopeful and the downtrodden,
Women and Children:	the lonely and the overwhelmed.
Leader:	Teach them your lessons of love.
Women and Children:	Strengthen their faith and their resolve to follow you.
Leader:	Bless them and help us to show them, and you, our gratitude for the gifts they are to us.
Leader:	We pray in Jesus's name.
Women and Children:	Amen.

At the Birth of a Baby

Author of Life, we thank you for the incomparable joy we feel at the arrival of _____.

We are grateful for his/her safe delivery and for those whose hands guided him/her into this world.

We pray that in the days ahead you will bless this child with knowledge of your love and grace.

May he/she be nurtured by caring parents, wise teachers, and devoted coaches.

May he/she grow to be strong, yet gentle; confident, yet kind; and show generosity of spirit and discipline of mind.

And for all his/her days, may he/she feel the presence of your Holy Spirit, leading him/her to an ever-growing awareness of your abiding love through Jesus Christ our Lord, in whose name we pray. Amen.

Prayer at the Start of the Sunday School Year

Holy God, as we begin another season of Christian education, we pray that you will guide and bless us. Thank you for those who have answered the call to share their time and their knowledge. Help them to impart an appreciation for the gift of your Word and a deeper understanding of who you are and who you call us to be. Shepherd our teachers as they prepare their lessons and as they instruct your disciples.

We thank you for our students, and we ask that you would help them to be attentive, faithful, and committed to learning. Let them find joy in discovering the depth of your love for them, and help them to support one another in and out of the classroom.

We thank you for the parents who have brought their children for instruction. May the lives they lead reinforce the lessons their children learn and encourage imitation of the example set by Jesus Christ, in whose name we pray. Amen.

Prayer for Graduates

God of Love, we give thanks

that these, our graduates, have found the success born of hard work

and have, by your grace, come to a new place in their life journeys.

We pray that as they move forward to new schools, new careers, and new adventures,

you will walk beside each of them.

They have acquired knowledge; now grant them wisdom to use that knowledge

in ways that give glory to you and in ways that fulfill your plan for their lives.

They have begun to claim a vision; give them eyes to see the way

to lasting joy and the abundant life.

When they are afraid, give courage; when they are lonely, grant comfort;

when they are uncertain, send your Spirit of Truth and Conviction to guide them.

Even as they commit their hearts, and their minds, and their lives to your generous care, may we be ever mindful of those ways that we, as your Body,

may show them your love, encourage them in their faith, and celebrate their gifts.

In Christ's name we pray. Amen.

Prayer for One Departing for College

Divine Teacher,

We ask that as your servant _____ begins a new leg on his/her educational journey,

you would bless him/her with the knowledge that you are with him/her.

Give direction to his/her academic efforts so that he/she may develop his/her gifts in ways that glorify you and fulfill your call on his/her life.

May his/her teachers be erudite, enthusiastic, and gracious;

May his/her fellow students be curious, companionable, and disciplined.

Help him/her to be confident as he/she faces the challenges before him/her.

Grant, O God, that we who have enjoyed his/her growth and have participated in helping him/her to prepare for this moment

may be steadfast in our continued nurturing of his/her development.

Keep us vigilant in praying for his/her needs,

attentive to his/her hopes and his/her concerns,

and faithful in our belief in his/her abilities.

We thank you for the gift that he/she has been to us, and we pray that he/she will continue to be a blessing to others as he/she is embraced by a new community.

Give wisdom to your servant, O God,

and educate him/her in the ways of Christian living and love.

We pray in Jesus' holy name. Amen.

Prayer for Those in Military Service

God of the Universe,

You have created us and called us into community

with you and one another,

a community of grace and love.

But your plan for us is not yet fully realized,

and your peace is not yet known in every place.

This day, as your children are called to take up arms,

We pray that you will give them guidance and protection.

Seal hope in their hearts and keep bitterness at bay.

Comfort them, and inspire them to comfort others

who know the fear of battle and the pain of loss,

whose families are worried, and whose lives are changed.

Help them to feel the support of those they leave behind,

as we, grateful for their sacrifices, continue to pray for them

and eagerly await their homecomings.

Give wisdom to those who face combat and to those who are entrusted with the leadership of troops and nations,

that justice and truth may put a swift end to war

and hasten the day when all your children will be reconciled

to one another and to you.

We pray in the name of the Prince of Peace,

our Lord and Savior, Jesus Christ. Amen.

Prayer for a Scouting Award Service

Loving God, you are the great Scoutmaster, and we give you thanks as we gather this day.

We thank you for the youth of our community—for their energy, their curiosity, and their desire to learn and grow.

We thank you for all those who dedicate themselves to the task of guiding children to adulthood—for family, friends, and community leaders who patiently share their knowledge and talents so that your plan for each youth might be realized.

We thank you for the blessings of Scouting, and for the many ways it serves our children and our nation.

And we thank you for the joy we feel as we celebrate the efforts of one who has taken to heart the law and the spirit of Scouting.

Be with us here as we reflect on the activities and achievements

that have brought us to this place,

and send your Spirit to guide us on the next leg of the journey.

We pray in your holy name. Amen.

Wedding Blessings

Hear now the blessing:

God of Love, we pray that you will bless _____ and _____ as they begin their life together as husband and wife. Grant that they will always feel your presence, guiding them and offering encouragement and reassurance. May each find in the other a confidante, companion, and comforter. May they love extravagantly, unconditionally, and enduringly. May their home be a place of peace, prosperity, and hospitality where grace, faith, and laughter abound. Grant them patience in difficult times, confidence in themselves and one another, and trust in you. Grant that they will always have the loving support of family and friends. And for all of their days may they hold fast to the hope, the desire, and the promises that unite them today. We pray in the name of Love Incarnate. Amen.

❧

Loving God, see before you your beautiful children, _____ and _____. Give to them your blessing as they are joined today as husband and wife. Be with them in the days ahead as they share life's journey. Encourage and rejoice with them in times of celebration, and strengthen and sustain them through whatever challenges they may face. Guide them as they make important decisions and surround them with family and friends who offer wise counsel and generous support. Help them to be faithful to the promises they have made this day, and let them never take for granted the gift you have given them in one another. Grant that they may care for each other with kindness and patience, may listen attentively to one another, and may share with one another hopes, goals, laughter, and longevity. Make their home a place of welcome and comfort where love abides and your grace is known. These things we pray, in Jesus's name. Amen.

A Wedding Grace

Dear God, we pray your blessing on _____ and _____ and on all here gathered in celebration of their union.

Grant that, through the years, they will know no hunger save that for your truth.

By your grace, multiply their faith and love as loaves and fishes.

Feed them daily with your wisdom and peace, and nurture their commitment to one another.

May this wedding feast we share strengthen us to serve you and yours, and may we receive these and all your gifts with grateful hearts.

In the name of Love Incarnate, we pray. Amen.

Prayer of Blessing on the Occasion of a Wedding Anniversary

God of Grace, we give thanks for the joy we feel as we gather to celebrate _____ and _____.

We thank you for the love that has joined this couple through their years of marriage,

and we ask that it would continue to grow in strength and beauty.

We pray that you will always bless their union with the compassion, humor, sharing, and caring that are the hallmarks of healthy relationships.

We ask that we might be an encouragement to them, even as they are an example to us.

We give thanks for the family and friends who grace their lives,

and we ask that you will keep their loved ones safe and healthy.

Give _____ and _____ much to celebrate in the years ahead,

and walk beside them always.

May all here gathered work to strengthen the ties of affection, respect, and devotion that unite us.

We give thanks and we celebrate, O God of Love, what you have put together and sustain,

and we pray that you will bless _____ and _____ with many more years of love, faith, and happiness.

In Christ's name, we pray. Amen.

For One Who Is Ill

Holy God, we ask that you would place your healing hand upon
_____ as he/she faces this time of illness. Help him/her to
know that he/she is not alone in his/her discomfort or distress but
that your Spirit of Restoration is with him/her. Allow _____
time for rest and recuperation, and send comforters to offer help
and reassurance.. Guide _____ through this challenging
time, and let him/her know the joy of recovered health. In Jesus's
name, we pray. Amen.

For One Facing Surgery

God of Hope and Healing, we ask that you will bless _____
as he/she prepares for surgery. Grant him/her confidence in the
plans that are being made for his/her care. Be with the doctors
who will serve him/her; guide their hands and give them wisdom
as they make important decisions. Be with the family and friends
who will care for _____ during his/her recuperation; help
them to be attentive, kind, and patient. We pray that in the days
ahead, _____ may enjoy a speedy and complete recovery
and, with a grateful heart, give thanks to you for your abundant
grace. In Jesus's name, we pray. Amen.

At the Death of a Loved One

Ruler of Heaven, we thank you for the gift of life as we remember the life of your servant, _____. We are grateful for the time we shared, for the memories we hold dear, and for the knowledge that, through Christ's grace and sacrifice, we may look forward to sweet reunion one day. We pray that, by your mercy, _____ is now resting peacefully in the everlasting arms that are the true home of all who put their faith and trust in you. Grant that we who mourn her/his passing may be comforted by the presence of your Holy Spirit, through Jesus, the Christ, in whose blessed name we pray. Amen.

Litany for a Funeral Service

Author of Life, we give thanks that you are a God who hears the cries of your children and promises to answer when we call upon you in faith. Guide us as we pray.

Leader: That _____ now knows the peace that surpasses all understanding and that she/he now sees clearly the loving face of the Creator, we pray to the Lord.

Congregation: Lord, hear our prayer.

Leader: That those who mourn may be comforted by the abiding presence of the Holy Spirit and by the friends and family who gather in Christ's name, we pray to the Lord.

Congregation: Lord, hear our prayer.

Leader: That our hurting world may be healed by the truth that gives us hope, the gospel of boundless grace and eternal life, we pray to the Lord.

Congregation: Lord, hear our prayer.

Leader: That we may, one day, share the cup of blessing with Christ, a cloud of witnesses, and one another in the kingdom of heaven, we pray to the Lord.

Congregation: Lord, hear our prayer.

Leader: Lord, hear our prayer and let our cry come to you. Hold us in your gentle arms and strengthen us as we await the coming of our Savior, Jesus Christ, in whose name we pray. Amen.

Prayer of Blessing for a New Home

Bless this home, O God, to be a place of welcome and refuge.

Let the light of your love flow through its windows,

and lock its doors against all that is displeasing to you.

Furnish these rooms with hope, peace, and faith in your providence;

and fill them with the sounds of laughter, caring conversation, and prayer.

Grant that those who reside here may know the gifts

of good health, good friends, and good times.

May their lives reflect their gratitude for the gift of a place to call home.

In Jesus's name, we pray.

Prayer for Those Moving Away

Loving God, we thank you for your servant(s) _____ and for his/her/their ministry among us.

Grant him/her/them journey mercies as he/she/they travel(s) to his/her/their new home and let him/her/them be warmly welcomed there.

Bless his/her/their new endeavors and provide him/her/them with the resources he/she/they need(s) to succeed.

Help him/her/them to build new relationships and give him/her/them opportunities to share his/her/their gifts in ways that show his/her/their love for you and his/her/their commitment to serve.

May he/she/they take along the memories of what we have shared, the affection we feel for him/her/them, and the knowledge that we will hold him/her/them in our hearts and in our prayers. In Jesus's name, we pray. Amen.

Prayer for Peacemaking

Leader: We gather here with the knowledge that God calls us to be peacemakers.

Congregation: We commit ourselves to do what we can to promote peace in our families, in our neighborhoods, and in our cities.

Leader: Where there is bullying and aggression,

Congregation: let us show a gentler, more loving way.

Leader: Where there is racism and religious intolerance,

Congregation: let us remember—and remind others—that we are all God's children.

Leader: May we, who are forgiven and blessed, bless others

Congregation: by being forgiving instead of bitter,

Leader: by seeking justice instead of revenge,

Congregation: and by embracing the hope of the future

Leader: instead of wallowing in despair over what was and is no longer.

All: In word and deed for all our days, let us declare our faith that by God's grace, peace may prevail upon the earth. Amen.

www.ingramcontent.com/pod-product-compliance
Lightning Source LLC
Chambersburg PA
CBHW071100090426
42737CB00013B/2408